C Programming for Beginners

Your Guide to Easily Learn C Programming In 7 Days

By iCodeAcademy

Table of Contents

INTRODUCTION:

In this day and age, nearly everyone has a computer and has access to the Internet. Each day, millions of people from different parts of the world go online to do a variety of activities, such as shopping, banking, downloading and sending data, reading and acquiring new information, doing online work, and communicating with other people.

When you go online, you see lots of different websites with different functionalities. Whatever your purpose for going to the Internet is, you will not be able to do it without using the program the Web developer or programmer has made. If you want to use and download an application, play a game, or perform an online task, you also need to use the program developed by the programmer.

Ubiquity of a Programming Language

With this being said, you can expect to see the C programming language live in action. In fact, this programming language is not only used online. It is also used in a variety of applications offline. The C language is widely popular and preferred by a lot of users because of its many advantages. It even beats other newer programming languages.

The C language is used for operating systems, assemblers, language compilers, text editors, network drivers, print spoolers, modern programs, language interpreters, data bases, and various utilities.

You may even be surprised to find out that many of the

applications you see and use today are based on the C language. For example, the Linux kernel was created using this programming language. Microsoft Windows also uses the NT kernel that was created with C and Assembly. In essence, every program that runs on Windows interact with the Windows API, which is actually an API based on the C language.

What's more, Android, Windows Phone, OSX, iOS, FreeBSD, and OpenBSD all use the C language at the core level of their architecture. This programming language is actually the most highly recommended system programming language.

A lot of operating systems are created using the C language. So, this means that each and every one of them provides an API that you can use to create platform-specific applications. Furthermore, a lot of embedded devices make use of the C language. It is also used to create interpreters.

Discovering the Expert's Tool of Choice

This programming language is chosen as the development language of many for certain reasons. For starters, it is the development language that programmers prefer for their operating systems such as Unix platforms as well as their variants. The C language is also chosen due to its low-level integration. So, if you want to inline an assembler, you can use this programming language to achieve your desired results.

Moreover, the C language is chosen by many programmers because of its cross-platform qualities. In fact, you can use it to create platform-independent codes. Then again, this may have been largely superseded by the Java programming language.

Nevertheless, the C language is still admired by many programmers and users because of its raw speed. A lot of programmers still believe that the C language is the best high-level programming language in terms of performance and speed. Thus, if you are primarily concerned with the performance of your program, you have to go for the C language to achieve your desired results.

Anyway, the C language is usually used along with C++. You can actually do a lot of things with these programming languages. You can create a wide variety of programs and applications. You can create systems for payroll and financial accounting, digital publishing, digital artwork and designs, COBOL converters, digital libraries, computerized displays, variable printing, application testing, RFID readers, and manufacturing resource planning.

An Ideal Reference for All Skill Levels

If you are in search of a material or reference that you can use to learn the C language, this book is highly recommended. It is perfect if you have to learn the programming language in the shortest amount of time possible. While it will not make you an instant expert, it will feed you with the basics that you need to go along with the learning process.

This book contains detailed information with regard to the C language and how you can create programs using it. It is carefully written in a way that everyone can easily understand and relate to. Names and terms are also explained so that you will not get lost when reading the book. So, even if you do not have any previous experience with computer programming, you will not experience headaches reading this.

This book is also designed for software programmers who want to learn the C programming language from scratch. It provides you with adequate understanding on the programming language. From there, you can bring yourself towards a higher level of expertise. While you are not really required to have any previous experience with computer programming, you still need to have a basic understanding of the terms commonly used in programming and computers.

You see, the C language is one of the most recommended computer programming languages for beginners. After all, it is a predecessor to many of the modern programming languages used today, such as Java and Python. In other words, before you can effectively learn these languages, you have to have a clear understanding of the C language first.

Through this book, you will learn how to write your first programs and see how they work in real time. You have to keep in mind that it is perfectly okay to make mistakes every now and then. It is through these mistakes that you learn. So, when you encounter an error on your program, you just have to study the part where you went wrong and redo it. When you run the programs in the C language, you will be notified in case you made a mistake. You will see the error and know which line you have to modify.

This book features Frequently Asked Questions (FAQ) sections that are written with beginners like you in mind. The author understands that beginners may have certain questions with regard to the elements of C that are not often discussed in books.

This book also teaches you how you can write the shortest programs possible, without negatively affecting your output. As a programmer, you want to make the most of your available time and space while still being efficient. You will also learn how to organize your codes and include remarks via comments so that you and your readers will not get confused.

Furthermore, this book discusses the topics involved in the C language in detail. Everything is explained thoroughly and clearly. This way, you can learn about them from the beginning until the end. It is not a good idea to just jump from one topic to another without understanding the other topics related to it first. However, you will also not take too much time since this book is intended to help you learn the C language in just 24 hours.

Even though there are really no pre-requisites to studying the C language, you will have a better chance of understanding it faster if you already read about similar programs such as C++. Just like C, C++ is also widely used for a variety of purposes. So, if you are planning to take on a programming career or create applications and software programs, it is highly recommended that you learn the C language.

Then again, this book is not just written for people who want to pursue a career in the field of information technology. You can also benefit from this book if you are a hobbyist programmer or you like to create programs for fun. You can also benefit from this book if you are a student who needs to take and pass a course related to this programming language. It will walk you from the fundamentals through the advanced topics.

Moreover, this book tells you about the advantages of learning the

C language. As you continue to read it and practice writing and running programs while using the examples as guidelines, you will have a better and clearer understanding of the programming language.

A Smart Choice of Knowledge Seekers

As you know, there are so many available computer programming languages you can use today. There are high level languages, such as Visual Basic, and low level assemblies. You can also find programming languages that are ideal for performing specialized tasks such as Python, Perl, and Ruby. Java is also great for performing a variety of tasks due to its huge API. Also, there are virtual machines that provide security elements. For instance, collecting garbage is a nice and useful feature that programmers can take advantage of.

The C language has been around for decades and has a lot of available source codes. You can learn a lot from it. Many of its issues have also been elucidated clearly. Through this book, you will learn about the principles applied in the C language. You will learn about the variable types, commands, and loop constructs among others.

Learning the C language is highly recommended because it allows you to work with bytes, individual bits, and pointers. You also get to learn more about optimization techniques. Plus, you get to see a bigger picture of more complex topics such as networking. Learning a high level language can make things easier for you. You can understand things so that you can fix them more efficiently.

The C language is a fun language to learn. For example, you can use it for data managers and system software. You can also use it for games and operating systems. Doing these things is much more difficult with Java and scripting languages. What's more, the C language makes your programs more aesthetically appealing.

You can really do a lot of things if you use the C language. With this book, you can succeed at making a lot of programs work. When you become adept at the C language, you can easily learn other languages and develop more applications.

Thanks again for downloading this book, I hope you enjoy it!

CHAPTER 1: INTRODUCTION TO C

THE C LANGUAGE

The C language was developed by Dennis MacAlistair Ritchie in 1972. It is a general purpose, imperative, and procedural programming language. It is mostly used on operating systems such as iOS and Windows. It is also one of the most popular computer languages of all time. It is practical and easy to learn. The programs are portable and the source code is compatible with many operating systems.

A Brief History of C

The development of the C language is closely related to that of the Unix operating system.

This programming language was developed by Dennis Ritchie in the 1970s. Ritchie was working at Bell Labs at that time. Before he came up with the C language, however, he worked on a project known as Multics, along with other people at Bell Labs.

Bell Labs is a research and scientific development company that is owned by Nokia, which is a Finnish company. Its roots are in the consolidation of some engineering departments at the Western Electric Company and the American Telephone & Telegraph company, also known as AT&T.

Anyway, during that time, Ritchie and his colleagues were working on the Multics project; they aimed to come up with an operating system that a huge computer can use. They wanted thousands of users to be able to benefit from their operating system project.

However, Bell Labs suddenly quit the project in 1969 because Ritchie and his colleagues cannot produce a system that is useful in the economic sense. Due to the failure of this project, they were forced to look for a new project that they can focus on. Ken Thompson and Dennis Ritchie were eager to start this new project.

Thompson started to work on developing a file system. In fact, he made a version of his new file system in the assembler, for the DEC PDP-7. This file system was used for Space Travel as well. It was a popular game during that time.

Eventually, the duo started to see improvements in their work. They also started to include expansions in the file system. Since they already acquired useful knowledge and experience from working on the Multics project, they were able to include useful features with ease. These new features made the system more efficient.

Soon enough, a complete system was done. Brian Kernighan, a computer scientist who also worked with Ritchie and Thompson at Bell Labs, called it UNIX. His name for the system was intended to be a sarcastic reference to the earlier Multics project. The entire system was written using assembly code.

Aside from FORTRAN and assembler, UNIX also featured an interpreter for the B programming language. It was directly derived from the Basic Combined Programming Language (BCPL), which was a structured, procedural, and imperative programming language that was designed by a computer scientist named Martin Richards.

The B language was developed by Ken Thompson in the late 1960s. During that time, computer codes were mainly written in assembly codes. So, each time a person wants to do a certain task, he has to write several pages of codes.

Since the B language was a high-level programming language, it provided a solution to this problem. Users no longer have to write several pages of code because they can simply write a few lines to complete their tasks. Writing a few lines of codes is definitely faster and more convenient.

The B language was further used for the development of UNIX. Due to its high level characteristics, users can easily write codes without wasting a lot of time. Then again, even though the B language seems to have a lot of advantages, it also has several disadvantages.

For instance, the B language did not know about data types. Programmers had to express everything in codes or machine words. In addition, the B language did not have structures. This became a problem for a lot of users.

So, Dennis Ritchie developed the C language in order to provide a solution to these problems. In the early 1970s, he converted the B language into the C language. He kept a lot of the syntax of the B language in their original form, but he added data types among other features.

The result was amazing. The C language had a high-level functionality and had the features necessary to program operating systems. Because of this, a lot of the components found in UNIX were rewritten using the C language. In fact, the UNIX kernel was rewritten on DEC PDP-11 in 1973.

Today, you can read all about the C language in the book entitled *The C Programming Language*. It was written by Ritchie and Kernighan. Kernighan made the world famous Hello World program as well as a lot of other programs in UNIX.

The first edition of The C Programming Language became the basis for many other books on the programming language. It actually became the standard of the C language. A committee was created by the American National Standards Institute (ANSI) in 1983. The objective of this committee was to create an up-to-date definition for the C language. By 1988, they were able to create the final standard definition of the language, which was called the ANSI C.

This final standard only had minor changes on the C language's original design because the old programs still had to work on the new standard. Then, the International Standards Organization (ISO) eventually adopted the ANSI C standard. Even though the standard should now be called ISO C, people are still used to calling it ANSI C.

Advantages of Using the C Language

There are a variety of computer programming languages you can choose from. Each one is unique in its own way. So, why should you go for the C language?

Programs written in C are fast.

You can go for newer programming languages such as Java and Python if you want to see a lot of features. However, if you want a C program that is fast, you should go for C. Its performance is still better due to the fact that it has less processing time.

Also, the C language allows for the direct manipulation of its hardware, which many high level programming languages do not offer. If you are a beginner, this is a huge advantage for you since you will be able to learn programming faster.

The standard programs are portable.

There is no need for you to write your program over and over.

Once you write a program on your computer, regardless of what operating system it has installed, you can compile it on another computer with a different operating system. For example, if you write it using Windows 7, you can compile it using Mac OS. The program will stay exactly the same. There would not be any unnecessary or unwanted changes.

Code sections can be stored for later use.

The concept of storing C code sections in libraries for later use is called modularity. These libraries are powerful. They can solve problems. For example, if you have to display an output, you can use the stdio.h library so you can use the printf ( ) function.

C can be used for a variety of purposes.

Even though it is one of the oldest programming languages, it is still preferred by a lot of programmers. It can be used for various applications, such as photo editing and system programming. It can also be used for embedded systems, databases, compilers, network drivers, print spoolers, and operating systems.

C is statically typed.

When you run a program in C, the variable type is not checked during run time. Instead, it is checked during compile time. Because of this, errors are quickly detected. Thus, you can develop your software with ease. In addition, a statically-typed language is faster than a dynamically-typed language.

C lets you understand how computers work.

When you learn the C language, you will not merely learn about programming, but you will also learn about the functionality of computers. For instance, you will be able to learn about memory allocation and management. You will also learn about computer architecture.

C precedes Python.

If you want to learn Python, which is also a great programming language for creating applications, you have to realize that learning C is necessary for learning Python. You will not be able to grasp Python interpreters if you do not know how to write and read C programs.

C is the basis for many other programming languages.

Python is not the only programming language that is related to C. C++, C#, and Java are also related to it. In fact, C++ is regarded as the superset of C. The syntax of PHP and JavaScript are also similar to that of C. So, if you become adept at writing programs in C, you will not have a hard time transitioning to these other programming languages.

Downsides to Using the C Language

Despite being the popular choice that it is, C isn't perfect. It does come with downsides that, while possibly minor for those simply curious or just beginning their programming pursuits, should be carefully taken into account by intermediate and advanced programmers.

C isn't capable of doing runtime checks by itself.

Runtime checking is quite an important feature as it immediately detects issues that occur when an application is run.

While someone with sufficient knowledge in the programming language shouldn't have much difficulty pinpointing problems that occur during runtime, having an internal mechanism that automatically checks for such defects would still prove to be advantageous – especially in minimizing the time needed to have a working program.

C doesn't support object-oriented programming.

Object-oriented programming (OOP) focuses on five key concepts: data abstraction, modularity, encapsulation, polymorphism, and inheritance. These make it possible to write applications that are easy to understand, manage, and maintain. OOP is innate to the C++ programming language and was mainly developed to overcome the limitations of–you've guessed it–the C programming language.

There's no variable type-checking in C.

When you've been writing an application for quite some time, you lose track of the types of certain variables. Unfortunately, given the age of the C programming language, it doesn't support variable type-checking – in other words, you're expected to keep track of such details on your own. If you fail to properly identify a particular variable for example, then the blame's entirely on you.

It should be pointed out, however, that some C enthusiasts are claiming that their favorite language, in its latest iteration (C11), finally supports type-checking albeit through a workaround.

Anything and everything can be done in C.

Clearly, complete and boundless flexibility in terms of purpose and application could be an advantage. However, in the case of programming, the lack of specialization can be deemed a downside. For example, if there's a language that's better suited to your goals, choosing to continue with C could only lead to an increase in the effort required to come up with something functional.

Still, even with the presence of better alternatives, knowing how to program in C should prove to be beneficial – as previously mentioned, it is similar to other popular, more recent languages.

RESERVED WORDS

Before you proceed with writing programs in the C language, you have to learn about the reserved words first. These words have specific purposes and cannot be used for any purpose other than what they are originally intended for.

The following reserved words are used in the C programming language:

auto – it is a storage class specifier used for declarations

break – it is a statement used for escaping from loops or switches

case – it is an option prefix used within the switch statement

char – it is a typename

continue – it is a statement used to branch towards the beginning of the next loop

default – it is an option used in the switch statement

double – it is a typename

do – it is a statement

else – it is a statement

entry – it is meant to be used in the future

extern – it is a storage class specifier

for – it is a statement

float – it is a typename

goto – it is a goto label

int – it is a typename

if – it is a statement

long – it is a typename

return – it is a functional statement

register – it is a storage class specifier

short – it is a typename

static – it is a storage class specifier

sizeof – it is a compile time operator

struct – it is a partial typename

typedef – it is a statement

switch – it is a statement

unsigned – it is a typename

union – it is a partial typename

while – it is a statement

void – it is a typename

enum – it is a partial typename, but only for ordinal types

const – it is a storage class specifier, but there is no allocated storage

volatile – it is a storage class specifier

signed – it is a typename

Preprocessor Directives

See to it that you also familiarize yourself with these preprocessor directives so that you can write working programs in the C language:

#include – it includes the file for the purpose of linking

#undef – it undefines a symbol that has been previously defined

#define – it defines a preprocessor symbol or macro

#if – it tests for conditional compilations

#ifndef – it tests for conditional compilations

#ifdef – it tests for conditional compilations

#endif – it tests for conditional compilations

#else – it tests for conditional compilations

#error – it is a tool for debugging

#line – it is a tool for debugging

Libraries and Header Files

The header file contains the macro definitions, variable declarations, function declarations, and type definitions that are used in relation with the standard library. They are used to supplement an object code library that is linked at a compile time for a standard library function. Keep in mind that there are library facilities that are not available if there are no included header files. Some of the most common names for header files include the following:

stdio.h – it is the standard input and output

math.h – it is used for mathematical definitions

ctype.h – it is a macro for the character types

Constants

Octal – it has a prefix of 0 and involves the characters 0 to 7

Integer – it involves the characters 0 to 9

Hexadecimal – it has a prefix of 0x and involves the characters 0 to 9. It can also use A to F or a to f.

Character – it is declared using single quotes

Explicit long – it means that hexadecimal or octal and integer types can be declared as long when you write the letter L right after your constant

Strings – they are written using double quotes

Float – it involves the characters 0...0 and one (.). It can also involve scientific notation exponents that are preceded by the uppercase letter E or the lowercase letter e.

Primitive Data Types

int – it is an integer type

char – it holds a character

long int – it is used for an integer that is no smaller than int

short int – it is used for an integer that is no larger than int

float – it is a floating point, which is used for real numbers long float – it is a double precision float

void – it does not hold any value and does not use any storage, except when it is used as a pointer

double – it is a double precision float

Storage Classes

const – it does not allocate any variable and the value does not change

auto – it is used for local variables

extern – it is used for a variable that has been defined in a different file

register – it is used for storing in the register as much as possible

static – it is used when a value has been preserved between function calls

volatile – it is used when a value is changeable by an agent outside of the program

Character Utilities

These are used when you use char ch; in your program.

isalpha (ch) – it means alphabetic order, from A to Z or a to z

islower (ch) – it means lower case

isupper (ch) – it means upper case

isxdigit (ch) – it covers the range of A to F or a to f or 0 to 9 isdigit (ch) – it covers the range of 0 to 9

isspace (ch) – it is a whitespace character

ispunct (ch) – it is symbolic or a punctuation

isalnum (ch) – it is alphanumeric

isgraph (ch) – it is used when the character can be printed or is printable

isprint (ch) – it is used when the character can be printed or is printable on screen and space

isascii (ch) – it is used within the range of 0 to 127

iscntrl (ch) – it is a control character and is not printable

iscsym (ch) – it is a valid character for the identifier in C

tolower (ch) – it converts the character to a lowercase letter

toupper (ch) – it converts the character to an uppercase letter

toascii (ch) – it converts the character to its ASCII equivalent

Special Control Characters

These characters are necessary in a program, even though they are not visible on your screen. They are used for specific purposes, such as for cursor movements. They are also written into ordinary characters or strings with the use of the backslash symbol (\ ) and another character.

The following are the special control characters used in the C programming language:

\b – it is the backspace

\f – it is the form feed

\n – it is the new line

\r – it is the carriage return

\t – it is the horizontal tab

\v – it is the vertical tab

\" – it is the double quotes character

\' – it is the single quote character

\\ – it is the backslash character

\ddd – it is the character ddd in which ddd is actually an ASCII code given in base 8 or octal

Input and Output Functions

It is important for you to take note of the following:

scanf ( ) – it means formatted input analysis

printf ( ) – it means formatted printing

putchar ( ) – it means putting one character in the stdout file buffer

getchar ( ) – it means getting one character from the stdin file buffer

puts ( ) – it puts the string in stdout

gets ( ) – it gets the string from stdin

fscanf ( ) – it means formatted input from the general files

fprintf ( ) – it means formatted printing to the general files fputs ( ) – it means putting the string in the file

fgets ( ) – it means getting the string from the file

fclose ( ) – it closes the file that was opened by fopen ( )

fopen ( ) – it opens or creates a file for a high level access

getc ( ) – it gets one character from the file

ungetc ( ) ; – it is used to undo the last get operation

fgetc ( ) – it gets the character from the file

putc ( ) – it puts the character to the file

fputc ( ) – it puts the character from the file

feof ( ) – it is the end of the file. It either returns false or returns true

fwrite ( ) – it writes a block of characters

fread ( ) – it reads a block of characters

fseek ( ) – it finds the position of the file

ftell ( ) – it returns the position of the file

fflush ( ) – it empties the file buffers

rewind ( ) – it moves the position of the file towards the beginning

creat ( ) – it creates a new file

close ( ) – it closes the file that has been opened with open ( )

open ( ) – it opens the file for low-level use

read ( ) – it reads a block of bytes that have not yet been translated

write ( ) – it writes a block of bytes that have not yet been translated unlink ( ) – it deletes the file

rename ( ) – it renames the file

lseek ( ) – it finds the position of the file

remove ( ) – it deletes the file

Conversion Specifiers

There is a specific set of conversion specifiers for printf and another specific set of conversion specifiers for scanf. You have to keep in mind that the conversion characters used for scanf are not the same as those used for printf. Hence, you have to be careful when using them in your program. See to it that you become familiar with the long types.

The following are the conversion specifiers for printf. You have to take note that the lowercase letter l may be used as a prefix for long types.

u – it means unsigned denary integer

d – it means signed denary integer

o – it means octal integer

x – it means hexadecimal integer

s – it means string

g – it means use e or f, whichever one is shorter

f – it means a fixed decimal floating point

c – it means a single character

e – it means scientific notation floating point

The following are the conversion specifiers for scanf:

ld – it means long int

d – it means denary integer

o – it means octal integer

x – it means hexadecimal integer

f – it means float type

h – it means short integer

lf – it means double or long float

e – it means float type

c – it means single character

le – it means double

s – it means character string

COMPILERS

A compiler is basically a program that translates a high-level language into another language, whether it is machine-specific or assembly. It also translates source codes or plain texts into object codes, which usually come in a form that is ideal for processing by linkers and other programs. Most programmers aim to translate their source code so that they can come up with an executable or working program.

When the compiler is done translating the source codes into object codes, the objects must be linked to the executable. You can do this by using a linker, which is a type of program. More often than not, the link stage and the compile stage are automatically performed. Then again, you have the option to perform the stages individually.

There are a lot of compilers available on the market today. Some of them are operating system specific, while others can be used on a variety of platforms.

GNU Compilers

The GNU Compiler Collection (GCC) features front ends for the C language as well as C++ and Objective – C and their respective libraries. The GCC may be used on various platforms. Nonetheless, it is most commonly used on Linux and UNIX.

If you wish to use the GCC on your windows machine, see to it that you check out Cygwin first. Do not worry because you are not restricted to installing a Windows partition alone. You may also use a Linux partition. Then again, keep in mind that it is strongly recommended for you to use Ubuntu distribution.

There are so many text editors you can find on the Internet. As the programmer, you are free to use any text editor you want to write your codes. Once you have finished your program, you may use the command below. This command will compile your program in the C language:

```
# gcc - o < name of output > < your - source.c >
```

CHAPTER 2: GETTING STARTED

HELLO WORLD!

The phrase "hello world" is often used in computer programs. It is simple and straightforward. It is usually used to show the syntax of the program. What better way to start writing programs than with a "hello world"?

Since you are a beginner, you should start with a basic program such as the following:

```c
#include < stdio.h >
main ( )
{
        // This sample program displays the output Hello World!
        /* This sample program displays the output Hello World!
*/
        /* This sample program displays the output
        Hello World! */
        printf ( "Hello World! \n" ) ;
        return 0 ;
}
```

When you run the above given sample code, you will get this output:

```
Hello World!
```

Now, let us discuss the parts and the elements you used in this sample program.

#include <stdio.h>

The stdio.h header file allows you to use the function printf ( ), which contains your text. Your compiler knows where to find it. In order for you to use this header file, you have to include it in the program. You can do this by using the preprocessor #include.

Keep in mind that the C language cannot really do much on its own, which is why you have to use files to run your program and get your desired output.

Then again, you do not necessarily need to use stdio.h all the time. You can use a different header file, depending on the requirements of your program. For instance, if you have to calculate a square root, you have to use sqrt ( ).

main ( )

The function main ( ) allows the code to be executed in the program. It does not really matter where you put it. The code will execute right where this function starts.

Aside from main ( ), you can also use int main ( ) or void main ( ), and you will get the same output. However, using void main ( ) is not recommended.

{ }

These curly braces contain the body of your main ( ) function.

//

This is a double slash comment prefix. You can use it to write a comment on a single line.

/ */*

These are a slash asterisk and an asterisk slash. You can use them to write a comment on a single line or on multiple lines.

printf( );

This library function sends the formatted output to your screen. It displays whatever you put within the quotation marks. Make sure that you do not forget to put the semicolon (;) at the end of your statement.

return 0;

The return statement ends your program. Unlike the function main ( ), the return statement is not mandatory. However, in the sample program shown above, return 0 is necessary. Otherwise, you will get an error. You can omit the return statement if you use int main ( ) or void main ( ) instead of main ( ). If you do not want to experience any issues, it is best to just use a return statement in all of your programs.

FREQUENTLY ASKED QUESTIONS (FAQ)

Is the C language case sensitive?

Yes, it is. Thus, you have to be careful with your use of uppercase and lowercase letters. For example, the words "Hello World", "hello world", and "HELLO WORLD" are all considered different in C. They may contain the same letters of the alphabet, but they are different in terms of their use of uppercase and lowercase letters. So, they would be read differently.

Who is the father of the C language?

Dennis MacAlistair Ritchie is the father of the C language. He was an American computer scientist who created the programming language.

Where did the C language get its name?

It was inspired by the B language, where it got many of its features.

The B language was developed by Dennis Ritchie, who also developed the C language, and Ken Thompson in the late 1960's. It was derived from the Basic Combined Programming Language (BCPL), which is a structured, procedural, and imperative programming language.

What is the difference between int main ( ) and void main ( )?

When you use int main ( ) , you have to end the program with a return 0 or the appropriate value. If you use void main ( ) , you will be able to skip a line.

Do you have to use return 0 all the time?

No. You can also use return 1, depending on your program. The return value generally indicates how your program should exit. The value 0 represents a normal exit for the function main ( ).

What is the difference between return and exit?

Return is used to exit from the function. Exit, on the other hand, is used to exit from the program.

FUNDAMENTALS

In this chapter of the book, you will learn about the basic elements of the C language.

Operators

In the C language, constants and variables are operated or controlled by the operators. The basic operators are generally the same as arithmetic operators.

The arithmetic operators include the plus sign (+) for performing addition, the asterisk (*) for performing multiplication, the minus sign (-) for performing subtraction, the forward slash symbol (/) for performing division, the percentage sign or the modulus (%) for finding the remainder, and the equal sign (=) for assigning expressions.

There are also other operators used for additional tasks. For instance, the iostream header lets you use the insertion operator (<<) if you want a certain output to be processed. You can also access other operators even if you do not use the #include directive. The basic operators are classified under comparison operators, increment and decrement operators, logical operators, and compound assignment operators.

Variable Declaration

Before you include variables in your operations, see to it that you declare them first. You also have to indicate their values. When you declare a variable, see to it that you use the following syntax:

```
type variable ;
```

See to it that you do not forget to specify the data type. You have to specify it, just like you do when you initialize functions. Thus, if you want to declare *w* as an integer variable type, you have to initialize it. You have to type the following:

```
int w ;
```

Once you have declared the integer w, you can allocate a specific value to it. You have to use the assign operator (=) to do this process. For example, if you want to assign the value *10* to the variable *w*, you should write the following:

```
w = 10 ;
```

You should always make sure that you declare the variable prior to assigning a value into it. Likewise, you have to declare your variable and allocate a value into it by using a single line. Take a look at the following example:

```
int w = 10 ;
```

Aside from using these expressions for your program, you may also want to consider using operators.

Increment and Decrement Operators

The increment operator consists of two plus signs (++). The decrement operator consists of two minus signs (- -). The primary purpose of these operators is to make the expression of adding and subtracting 1 from the variable faster. It becomes shorter so that you can save space in your program. You will also spend less time and energy when writing your code. For example, you can write the following statement:

if w = 4 , then + + w must be equal to 5 while - - w must be equal to 3.

As the programmer, you can include the increment and decrement operators as either a suffix or a prefix in your program. This is useful and practical if you want to identify the values of two or more variables.

Then again, you have to keep in mind that when you use the increment and decrement operators as suffices (x++ or x - -), the original value of x prior to the addition or subtraction of 1 would be denoted. If you run the operators on their own, both the x++ and the ++x would have a similar meaning. Conversely, if you use it in setting other variables, you would see their obvious differences.

```
a = 5 ;
b = ++a ;
```

As you can see in the example shown above, the value of b is determined only after the value of a is raised. Thus, the value of b eventually becomes 6.

```
a = 5 ;
b = a++ ;
```

Still using the same example shown above, you can see that the value of b is determined before the value of a is increased. Thus, the value of b eventually becomes 6.

Compound Assignment Operators

Aside from the standard assignment operator (=) and the basic arithmetic operators, you can also use compound assignment operators to perform operations before you assign values in your program. These operators are shortened versions of the usual expressions involved in basic arithmetic operators.

x + = 1 ;   // It is practically the same as the expression x = x + 1 ;

x - = 1 ;   // It is practically the same as the expression x = x – 1 ;

x * = y ;   // It is practically the same as the expression x = x * y ;

x /= y ;   // It is practically the same as the
expression x = x / y ;

Arithmetic Operators

Operators	Descriptions
Addition (+)	It adds the operands.
Subtraction (-)	It subtracts the second operand from the previous one.
Multiplication (*)	It multiples both operands.
Division (/)	Divides operands (first by second)
Modulus (%)	It divides the first operand by the second operand and returns the remainder
Increment Operator (++)	It increases the integer value by one.
Decrement Operator (--)	It decreases the integer value by one.

Assignment Operators

Operators	Descriptions
=	It is a simple assignment operator that allocates a value from the right side operand to the left side operand.
+=	It is an add AND assignment operator that adds the right operand and the left operand together, and then allocates the resulting value to the left operand.
-=	It is a subtract AND assignment operator that subtracts the right operand from the left operand, and the allocates the resulting value to the left operand.
*=	It is a multiply AND assignment operator that multiplies the right operand with the left operand, and then allocates the resulting value to the left operand.
/=	It is a divide AND assignment operator that divides the left operand with the right operand, and then allocates the resulting value to the left operand.
%=	It is a modulus AND assignment operator that takes the modulus by using two operands and assigning the resulting value to the left operand.
<<=	It is a left shift AND assignment operator.
>>=	It is a right shift AND assignment operator.
&=	It is a bitwise AND assignment operator.
^=	It is a bitwise exclusive OR and assignment operator.
|=	It is a bitwise inclusive OR and assignment operator.

Relational Operators

Operators	Descriptions
==	It verifies if the values are equal.
!=	It verifies if the values are not equal.
>	It verifies if the value of the first is greater than that of the second.
<	It verifies if the value of the first is less than that of the second.
>=	It verifies if the value of the first is greater than or equal to that of the second.
<=	It verifies if the value of the first is less than or equal to that of the second.

Logical Operators

Operators	Descriptions
&&	It is the logical AND operator. In the event that both operands are non-zero, the condition is true.
||	It is the logical OR operator. In case one of two operands is non-zero, the condition is true.
!	It is the logical NOT operator. It reverses the operand's logical state. In case the condition is found to be true, this operator makes it false.

Bitwise Operators

Operators	Descriptions
& (binary AND)	It copies the bit if it is present in both operands.
| (binary OR)	It copies the bit if it is present in either operand.
^ (binary XOR)	It copies the bit if it is present in one operand, but not both.
~ (binary ones complement)	It flips bits.
<< (binary left shift)	It moves the value of the left operand towards the left based on the number of bits assigned by the right operand.
>> (binary right shift)	It moves the value of the left operand towards the right based on the number of bits assigned by the right operand.

To help you understand the concept of operators better, you have to take a look at the following examples.

In this sample program, you will see how arithmetic operators are used.

// This sample program shows you how arithmetic operators are used.

```c
#include < stdio.h >
int main ( )
{
        int a = 11 , b = 3 , c ;

        c = a + b ;
        printf ( " a + b = %d \n " , c ) ;

        c = a - b ;
        printf ( " a - b = %d \ n " , c ) ;

        c = a * b ;
        printf ( " a * b = %d \ n " , c ) ;

        c = a / b ;
        printf ( " a / b = % d \ n " , c ) ;

        c = a % b ;
        printf ( " This is the remainder that you get when you divide
a with b : %d \ n " , c ) ;

return 0 ;
}
```

When you run the above given sample program, you will get the following output:

a + b = 14

a - b = 8

a * b = 33

a / b = 3

This is the remainder that you get when you divide a by b : 2

As you can see in the output shown above, all of the operators used in the program performed their specific tasks, which are addition, subtraction, multiplication, and division respectively.

However, if you divide 11 by 3, you will get an answer of 3.67. This is why you got 3 in your output. You got this value because variable a and variable b are both integers. So, it is only appropriate that you also get an integer for your output. The compiler does not read the terms after the decimal point, and that is why it only displayed 3 instead of 3.67.

Then, the modulo operator (%) calculates the remainder of a and b. If you divide 11 by 3, you will get a remainder of 2. You can use the modulo operator when you compute for integers alone.

To help you understand this concept further, here is another example that you can check out:

For example, you have the following variables and values in your program:

a = 5.0

b = 2.0

c = 5

d = 2

In the C language, the following operators are used to compute for their values:

a / b = 2.5 // You get this output because the two operands are both floating-point variables

c / b = 2.5 // You get this output because one of the operands is a floating-point variable

a / d = 2.5 // You get this output because one of the operands is a floating-point variable c / d = 2 // You get this output because the two operands are both integers

In this next example, you will learn about decrement and increment operators. The following sample program shows you how these operators function in a program.

```
// This is a sample program that demonstrates how decrement and
increment operators work

#include < stdio.h >
int main ( )
{
        int a = 10 , b = 100 ;
        float c = 10.5 , d = 100.5 ;

printf ( " ++a = %d \n " , ++a ) ;
printf ( " - - b = %d \n " , - - b ) ;
printf ( " ++c = %d \n " , ++c ) ;
printf ( " - - d = %d \n " , - - d ) ;
return 0 ;
}
```

When you run the above given sample program, you will get the following output:

```
++a = 11

- - b = 99

++c = 11.500000

++d = 99.500000
```

As you can see in the output, the operators - - and ++ are used as prefixes. However, they can also be used as postfixes such as a- - and a++.

In the C language, the increment operator (+ +) increases the value of the variable by 1. On the other hand, the decrement operator (- -) decreases the value of the variable by 1.

To help you understand this concept further, you have to take a look at the following examples:

For instance, you have a = 5. This gives you the following values:

++a ;   // a turns into 6

- - a ;   // a turns into 6

a++ ;   // a turns into 7

a - - ;   // a turns into 5

So, how does using the ++ operator and the - - operator differ when they are used as a prefix and a postfix?

For instance, if you use the ++ operator to serve as a prefix like in ++var, you get a value that is incremented by 1. A value is then returned.

On the other hand, if you use the ++ operator to serve as a postfix like in var++, you see that the original value of var gets returned first. Var is also incremented by 1.

To help you understand this concept further, you have to take a look at the following sample program:

```c
#include < stdio.h >
int main ()
{
        int var = 7 ;

// The value is shown and then var gets increased to 8

printf ( " %d \n " , var ++ ) ;

// At first, var is equal to 8. Then, it gets increased to 9 and is
shown at the output

printf ( " %d " , ++var ) ;

return 0 ;
}
```

When you run the above given sample program, you will get the following output:

```
7

9
```

In the C programming language, you will also encounter relational operators. You have learned about these operators earlier in this book. However, in order for you to understand the concept further, you have to take a look at the following examples.

```c
// This sample program shows you how arithmetic operators work

#include < stdio.h >
int main ()
{
        int x = 5 , y = 5 , z = 10 ;
```

```
        printf ( " %d == %d = %d \n " , x , y , x == y ) ;      //
This one is true

        printf ( " %d == %d = %d \n " , x , z , x == z ) ;      //
This one is false

        printf ( " %d > %d = %d \n " , x , y , x > y ) ;      //
This one is false

        printf ( " %d > %d = %d \n " , x , z , x > z ) ;      //
This one is false


        printf ( " %d < %d = %d \n " , x , y , x < y ) ;      //
This one is false

        printf ( " %d < %d = %d \n " , x , z , x < z ) ;      //
This one is true

        printf ( " %d != %d = %d \n " , x , y , x != y ) ;      //
This one is false

        printf ( " %d != %d = %d \n " , x , z , x != z ) ;      //
This one is true

        printf ( " %d >= %d = %d \n " , x , y , x >= y ) ;      //
This one is true

        printf ( " %d >= %d = %d \n " , x , z , x >= z ) ;      //
This one is false


        printf ( " %d <= %d = %d \n " , x , y , x <= y ) ;      //
This one is true

        printf ( " %d <= %d = %d \n " , x , z , x <= z ) ;      //
This one is false

return 0 ;
```

```
}
```

When you run the above given sample program, you will obtain the following output:

```
5 == 5 = 1

5 == 10 = 0

5 > 5 = 0

5 > 10 = 0

5 < 5 = 0

5 < 10 = 1

5 != 5 = 0

5 != 10 = 1

5 >= 5 = 1

5 >= 10 = 0

5 <= 5 = 1

5 <= 10 = 1
```

In the C language, logical operators are also used. In the following sample program, you will learn how they function.

```
// This sample program shows you how logical operators work.

#include < stdio.h >
int main ()
{

    int x = 5 , y = 5 , z = 10 , result ;
```

```
    result = ( x = y ) && ( z > y ) ;

    printf ( " ( x = y ) && ( z > y ) is equal to %d \n " , result );
    result = ( x = y ) && ( z < y ) ;

    printf ( " ( x = y ) && ( z < y ) is equal to %d \n " , result );
    result = ( x = y ) || ( z < y ) ;

    printf ( " ( x = y ) || ( z < y ) is equal to %d \n " , result );
    result = ( x != y ) || ( z < y ) ;

    printf ( " ( x != y ) || ( z < y ) is equal to %d \n " , result );
    result = ! ( x != y ) ;

    printf ( " ! ( x == y ) is equal to %d \n " , result ) ;
    result = ! ( x == y ) ;

    printf ( " ! ( x == y ) is equal to %d \n " , result ) ;

return 0 ;
}
```

When you run the above given sample program, you will get the following output:

```
( x = y ) && ( z > y ) is equal to 1

( x = y ) && ( z < y ) is equal to 0

( x = y ) || ( z < y ) is equal to 1

( x != y ) || ( z < y ) is equal to 0

! ( x != y ) is equal to 1

! ( x == y ) is equal to 0
```

As you can see in the output of the sample program shown above, (x = y) && (z > 5) results in 1 due to the fact that the operand (x = y) and the operand (z > y) are both equivalent to 1, which is true.

You can also see that (x = y) && (z < y) results in 0 due to the fact that the operand (z < y) is equivalent to 0, which is false.

You can also see that (x = y) || (z < y) results in 1 due to the fact that the operand (x = y) is equivalent to 1, which is true.

You can also see that (x != y) || (z < y) results in 0 due to the fact that the operand (x != y) and the operand (z < y) are both equivalent to 0, which is false.

You can also see that !(x != y) results in 1 due to the fact that the operand (x != y) is equivalent to 0, which is false. Thus, the operand !(x != y) is equivalent to 1, which is true.

You can also see that the operand !(x == y) results in 0 due to the fact that the operand (x == y) is equivalent to 1, which is true. Thus, the operand !(x == y) is equivalent to 0, which is false.

You know, in the C language, there are other operators that you may have not yet heard about.

Comma Operator

This operator is used to connect expressions that are related to one another. To help you understand the concept of this operator further, you have to take a look at the following sample code:

int a , c = 3 , d ;

SizeOf Operator

This operator is a unary operator that returns the data size, such as that of variables, constants, arrays, and structures among others. To understand the concept of this operator further, you have to take a look at the following sample program:

```
#include < stdio.h >
int main ()
{
        int a , e [ 10 ] ;
        float b ;
        double c ;
        char d ;

        printf ( " The size of the int is %lu bytes \n " , sizeof ( a ) ) ;
        printf ( " The size of the float is %lu bytes \n " , sizeof ( b ) ) ;
        printf ( " The size of the double is %lu bytes \n " , sizeof ( c ) );
        printf ( " The size of the char is %lu byte \n " , sizeof ( d ) ) ;
        printf ( " The size of the integer type array that has 10 elements is
%lu bytes \n " , sizeof ( e ) ) ;

return 0 ;
}
```

When you run the above given sample program, you will obtain the following output:

The size of the int is 4 bytes

The size of the float is 4 bytes

The size of the double is 8 bytes

The size of the char is 1 byte

The size of the integer type array that has 10 elements is 40 bytes

Ternary Operator / Conditional Operator

This operator is a conditional operator. It is used for three operands. When you use this operator, you have to use the characters (?:).

The syntax of a conditional operator is as follows:

conditionalExpression ? expression 1 : expression2

The first expression, which in the above given example is conditionalExpression, gets evaluated first. If it is true, it gets evaluated to 1. If it is false, it gets evaluated to 0.

If the expression conditionalExpression is found to be true, expression1 gets evaluated. However, if the same expression is found to be false, expression2 gets evaluated.

To help you understand the concept of conditional operators further, you have to take a look at the following sample program:

```
#include < stdio.h >
int main ()
{
        char February ;
        int days ;
        printf ( " If the current year is a leap year, you have to enter
the value of 1. Otherwise, you have to enter any other integer value.
Input :  ") ;
        scanf ( " %c " , &February ) ;

// If the test condition ( February == ' 1 ' ) is found to be true,
then the days are equal to 29.
// If the test condition ( February == ' 1 ' ) is found to be false,
then the days are equal to 28.

        days = ( February == ' 1 ') ? 29 : 28 ;
        printf ( " The number of days in the month of February is
%d " , days ) ;

return 0 ;
}
```

When you run the above given sample program, you will obtain the following output:

If the current year is a leap year, you have to enter the value of 1. Otherwise, you have to enter any other integer value. Input : 1

The number of days in the month of February is 29

CHAPTER 3: FLOW OF CONTROL

STATEMENTS

The execution of a program is controlled by statements. An execution is called an iteration. In general, there are three statements used for looping: for, while, and do.

The For Statement

It allows you to repeat compound statements or statements for a certain duration. Its body is executed at least zero times and continues until the optional condition is found to be false. If you want to change and initialize values during your execution of your for statement, you may use optional expressions.

The syntax of the for statement is as follows:

for (init – expressionopt ; cond – expressionopt ; loop – expressionopt) statement

The execution of the for statement is done through the following steps:

If there is an init – expression, it gets evaluated in order for it to specify the initialization of the loop. A type of the init – expression does not have any restrictions.

If there is a cond – expression, it gets evaluated. It needs to have a pointer or arithmetic type. It also has to be evaluated right before every iteration. If you do that, you can achieve any of the following results:

If the cond – expression is found to be true or non-zero, then the statement gets executed. If there is a loop – expression, it gets evaluated. This loop – expression gets evaluated after every iteration. Keep in mind that this type does not have any restrictions. The side effects generally take place in a certain order. Then, the process will start once more alone with evaluation of the cond – expression.

In case the cond – expression gets skipped, then this cond – expression will be regarded as true. The execution will then continue. You have to take note that a for statement that does not have any cond – expression argument only terminates when a return or break statement within a statement body gets executed. The same thing happens when goto gets executed.

In case the cond – expression is found to be false or zero, the execution of for statement is terminated and the control is passed on towards the following program statement.

You have to keep in mind that the for statement can also be terminated when a return, break, or goto statement in your statement body gets executed.

In the for loop, the loop – expression is evaluated when there is a continue statement involved. If the break statement inside the for loop is executed, the loop – expression does not get executed or evaluated. The statement for (; ;) is actually a traditional way to come up with the infinite loop. You can only terminate this loop with the use of a return, break, or goto statement.

In order for you to understand this concept better, you have to take a look at the following example:

```c
// This sample program shows you how for statement works in the
C language

int main ()
{
        char * line = " He \t1 \t1 o Sample \ 0 ";
        int space = 0 ;
        int tab = 0 ;
        int i ;
        int max = strlen ( line ) ;
        for ( i = 0 ; i < max ; i++ )
{
        if ( line [ i ] == ' ')
        {
                space++ ;
        }
        if ( line [ i ] == ' \t ')
        {
                tab++ ;
        }
}
printf ( " The number of spaces is %i \n " , space ) ;
printf ( " The number of tabs is %i \n " , tab ) ;
return 0 ;
}
```

When you run the above given sample program, you will obtain the following output:

The number of spaces is 4

The number of spaces is 2

The While Statement

It allows you to repeat the statement until the specified expression turns out to be false. This statement has the following syntax:

The iteration statement:

while (expression) statement

Keep in mind that your expression has to have a pointer or arithmetic type. When everything is ready, your program will be executed through the following steps:

The expression gets evaluated first. If it is found to be false, then the body of the white statement does not execute. Instead, the control is passed from the while statement towards the next statement in your program. In case the expression is found to be true, which is represented by a non-zero, the statement body gets executed. The same process that was done before occurs once more.

You have to keep in mind that the while statement may also be terminated if a return, break, or goto gets executed within the body of the statement.

You have to make use of the continue statement if you want to end an iteration without needing to exit your while loop. Then, the continue statement passes the control towards the next iteration of your while statement.

In order for you to understand this concept further, you have to take a look at the following example:

```
while ( i >= 0 )
{
        string1 [ i ] = string2 [ i ] ;
        i - - ;
}
```

As you can see in the above given example, the characters from the string2 to the string1 are copied. So, if i is found to be greater than or equal to the value of 0, the value of string2 [i] gets allocated to string1 [i] and then i gets decremented. If i reaches or goes below 0, the execution of the statement is terminated.

The Do Statement

It keeps on executing until the condition is found to be false. This statement has the following syntax:

```
do statement while ( expression ) ;
```

Keep in mind that this statement is repeatedly executed for as long as the value of the expression stays non-zero. Such expression gets evaluated after every iteration. This is necessary in order for the loop to execute the statement one or more times.

With regard to the parentheses found around the expression, they are mandatory. If you do not include them in your statements, you will get an error when you try to run your program.

In addition, you have to take note that do is the sole control structure in the C programming language that explicitly ends with a semicolon (;). The other control structures in the C programming language tend to end with a statement. This means that they implicitly feature a closing brace or semicolon.

In order for you to understand this concept better, you have to take a look at the following example. In this example, the scalar product of two vectors are calculated with the use of the do statement:

```
w = 0 ; i = 0 ;
do
{
        w += a [ i ] * b [ i ] ;
        i++ ;
}
while ( i < n ) ;
```

Decision-Making Statements

When writing your programs in the C language, always remember that you need to specify at least one condition for testing or evaluation of the structures. You also have to include at least one statement for execution in case your condition is found to be true. You may include optional statements in case the condition is found to be false.

The flow diagram of the general form of a decision-making structure is as follows:

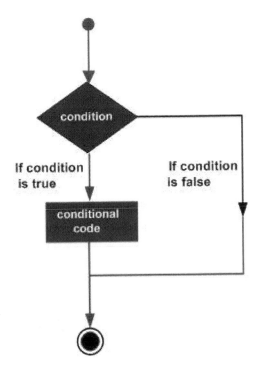

In the C language, you have to use the following types of decision-making statements in your programs:

Statements	Descriptions
if statement	It consists of a Boolean expression and at least one more statement.
if . . . else statement	It is followed by an optional else statement that executes if a Boolean expression is found to be false.
switch statement	It allows the variable to be tested for equality against a set of values.
nested if statement	A single if or else if statement can only be used within another if or else statement.
nested switch statement	A switch statement can only be used within another switch statement.

The If Statement

It consists of a Boolean expression, and then followed by at least one more statement. It has the following syntax:

```
if ( Boolean expression )
{
// This statement will be executed if the Boolean expression is found to be true.
}
```

You have to take note that the expression found within the parentheses can be anything. For instance, if its value is zero, the expression is considered to be false and the statement is ignored. If its value is a non-zero, the expression is considered to be true and the statement is executed.

In case the Boolean expression is found to be true, the block of code within the *if statement* gets executed. On the other hand, if it is false, the initial series of code after the end part of the *if statement* gets executed.

The flow diagram for the *if statement* is as follows:

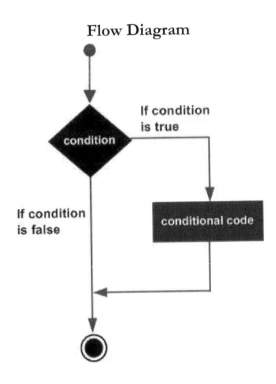

Flow Diagram

The *if statement* lets you test for different types of conditions, as well as branch out to different areas in the body of the program, based on your output.

```
if ( LargeNumber > SmallNumber )
LargeNumber = SmallNumber ;
```

AS you can see in the above given sample code, the elements LargeNumber and the SmallNumber are compared to each other. If the LargeNumber is proven to be larger, then the second line sets the value to the value of the SmallNumber, regardless of what it is.

```
if ( expression )
{
FirstStatement ;
SecondStatement ;
ThirdStatement ;
}
```

Advanced If Statements (Nested If Statements)

As the programmer, you are allowed to use any statement within an *if* or *else* clause, as well as within another *if* or *else* statement. However, you should remember that you are dealing with complex *if* statements when you see this format:

```
if ( expression1 )
{
if ( expression2 )
statement ;
else
{
if ( expression3 )
statement2 ;
else
statement3 ;
}
}
else
statement4 ;
```

If the two expressions are found to be true, the first statement gets executed. If the first and third expressions are found to be true and the second expression is false, the second statement gets executed. If your first expression is found to be true, but the second and third expressions are found to be false, the third statement gets executed. Lastly, if your first expression is found to be false, the fourth statement gets executed.

Nested If Statements and Braces

As a programmer, you have to be cautious when you use nest *if* statements in your programs.

```
if ( a > b )        // If a is found to be bigger than b
if ( a < c )        // and if a is found to be smaller than c
a = b ;             // then you should set a to the value of c
```

You have to avoid assigning *else* statements to the incorrect *if* statements. Moreover, you should always use whitespaces and indentions in your programs so that they will appear more organized and easier to read.

The If . . . Else Statement

Always keep in mind that the *if* statements may be followed by *else* statements, which execute if the Boolean expressions are proven to be false. The *if . . . else statement* has this syntax:

```
if ( Boolean_expression )
{
// The statement executes if the Boolean expression is found to be
```

```
true
}
else
{
// The statement executes if the Boolean expression is found to be
false
}
```

If your Boolean expression is proven to be *true*, the *if block* of code gets executed. Otherwise, the *else block* of code is the one that gets executed. The flow diagram of the *if . . . else statement* is as follows:

Flow Diagram

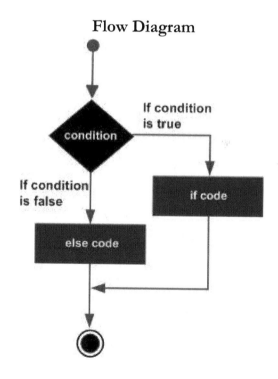

The If . . . Else If . . . Else Statement

If statements can be followed by *else if* . . . *else* statements. These statements are useful for testing different conditions with the use of the single *if* . . . *else* if statement. Each moment you use an *if* . . . *else if* . . . *else* statement, you have to make sure that you keep these pointers in mind:

- The if statement can have 0 or 1 else statement that must come after else if.
- The if statement can have 0 or as many else if statements that must go before the else.
- When an else if statement executes with success, no other else if or else must be tested.

The *if* . . . *else if* . . . *else* statement has this syntax:

```
if ( first Boolean expression )
{
// It executes when the first Boolean expression is true
}
else if ( second Boolean expression )
{
// It executes when the second Boolean expression is true
}
else if ( third Boolean expression )
{
// It executes when the third Boolean expression is true
}
else
{
// It executes when none of the above conditions is true.
}
```

The Nested Switch Statement

As the programmer, you are free to use a switch as part of the statement sequence of your outer switch. There are at least two hundred and fifty-six levels of nesting that you can use for your switch statements.

The Switch Statement

The *switch* statement allows for all variables to be tested for equality. A value is referred to as a case. In every case, the variable that gets switched on needs verification.

```
switch ( expression )
{
case constant – expression :
statement ( s ) ;
break ; // This is optional
case constant – expression :
statement ( s ) ;
break ; // This is optional
// You are free to use any number of case statements
default : // This is optional
statement ( s ) ;
}
```

Each time you use a *switch* statement, you need to remember these tips:

- All the expressions used in your switch statements must have enumerated or integral types.

- Any number of case statements may be used within a switch, as long as you include the value you used to compare the case. Make sure that you also include a colon.

- You have to use a constant expression of the same data type as the variable of the switch. It also has to be either a literal or a constant.

- In case the variable you switch on is equal to a case, the rest of the statements that follow it have to be executed until your program reaches a break statement.

- When your program finally reaches a break statement, it will terminate the switch. Then, the control flow moves on to the next line that follows your switch statement.

- There is no need for you to include a break in all of your codes or programs. If you do not see any break in the program, it means that the control flow continues to the next cases until the program reaches a break statement.

- You can use a default case in your switch statement. Since it is optional, you can just skip using it. Then again, if you ever decide to use it, make sure that you place it at the end of your switch.

The following figure is the flow diagram of a switch statement:

Flow Diagram

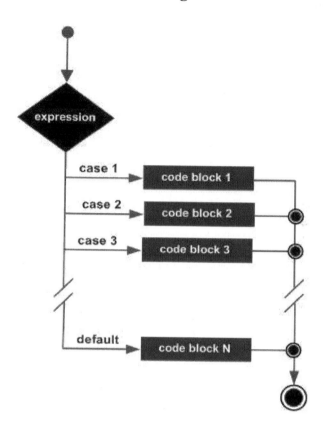

CHAPTER 4: ARRAYS

ELEMENTS OF ARRAYS

Arrays are practically collections of locations of data storage that hold a similar class of data. A storage location is called an *element of the array*. Declaring arrays is done by determining and writing their types, names, and subscripts.

The subscripts are the numbers of elements found within the array. They have square brackets.

long LongArray [20] ;

In the above given sample statement, you can see that a declaration of an array consisting of 20 long integers that is named LongArray is made. When your compiler reads it, it prepares the memory to hold twenty elements. You should take note that a long integer needs four bytes. In this particular declaration, a hundred contiguous bytes of memory will be prepared.

Elements of an Array

The elements of an array can be accessed through the offsets of names. Then, they are counted, starting from zero. This explains why the first element of an array is given a 0 value. For example, you can write ArrayName [0] .

If you choose to use the name LongArray, your first array element would be LongArray [0] while your second array element would be LongArray [1]. You will continue to count from that value until you reach your target destination.

SomeArray [3] , for example, has three elements, as you can tell by the value enclosed within its brackets. These elements are named SomeArray [0] , SomeArray [1] , and SomeArray [2] . SomeArray [n] also contains numbered elements from SomeArray [0] until SomeArray [n – 1] . So, LongArray [25] is numbered from LongArray [0] until LongArray [24] .

Writing Past the End of Arrays

Once you put sample values in the elements of the array, the compiler will start to calculate where it should store these values. It considers the sizes and subscripts of these values too.

For example, if you wish to write over a value that you stored at LongArray [5] , your compiler will multiply the offset according to the size of the element you used. In this example, the values you have are 5 and 4, respectively. It also moves 20 bytes from the beginning of the array as well as write the new values on the same location.

Then again, if you would rather write at LongArray [50] , your compiler will compute the distance of your first element. Then, it will write over any value it sees on that location. This is not a good outcome because writing a new value like this may only cause your program to have unpredictable results.

Array Initialization

When you declare an array, you may initialize it as a simple array, such as characters and integers. See to it that you never forget to include the equal sign (=). You also have to include a series of values that are separated by commas. Always remember that you have to enclose everything within braces.

Take a look at the following example:

```
int IntegerArray [ 5 ] = { 10, 20, 30, 40, 50 } ;
```

In the above given sample statement, the IntegerArray is declared as an array with five integers. It allocates the value of 10 to IntegerArray [0] and the value of 20 to IntegerArray [1] . The same process of allocating values goes on and on until the last IntegerArray. If you skip the array size, you produce an array that is big enough for initialization.

To understand this concept further, you have to take a look at this example:

```
int IntegerArray [] = { 10, 20, 30, 40, 50 } ;
```

When you write this, you create the same exact array that you have already created before.

If you wish to determine the array size of your program, you can command the compiler to compute it. You can input the following, for example:

```
const USHORT IntegerArrayLength ;
IntegerArrayLength = sizeof ( IntegerArray ) / sizeof (
IntegerArray [ 0 ] ) ;
```

As you can see in the sample code shown above, the constant USHORT variable IntegerArrayLength is set to whatever result you get from dividing the whole array size by the individual array size. Whatever value of the quotient you get is the number of array members.

Keep in mind that you are not allowed to initialize elements that you have declared for your array.

Consider the following example:

```
int IntegerArray [ 5 ] = { 10, 20, 30, 40, 50, 60 } ;
```

If you type this code, you will only generate a compiler error. This happens because you declared an array that has five members when you only initialized an array that has six values.

Take a look at this other example:

```
int IntegerArray [ 5 ] = { 10, 20 } ;
```

The above given example is allowed to be used in the C programming language. Even if uninitialized array members do not have guaranteed values, the aggregates are still initialized to 0. If you do not initialize the array member, the value would be set to 0.

You should allow the compiler to set your initialized array size. Keep in mind that it is not good practice to write beyond the end part of your array. Just like with variables, see to it that you use sensible names for your arrays in order to avoid confusion and misunderstandings. Also, you have to remember that the initial array member is always at offset 0.

Array Declaration

As the programmer, you are free to use any legal variable name you want for your array. However, you should avoid using a name that is the same as that of another variable and an array within the scope.

When you declare arrays, you must define the type of object stored, the name of your array, and a subscript that contains the number of objects to be held in the array at all times. Take a look at the following examples to understand the concept further:

```
int MyIntegerArray [ 90 ] ;

long * ArrayOfPointersToLongs [ 100 ] ;
```

If you decide to access the members of an array, you can use the subscript operator.

Again, consider the following examples:

int theNinthInteger = MyIntegerArray [8] ;

long * pLong = ArrayOfPointersToLongs [8]

All the arrays are counted starting from zero. The arrays of *n* items are numbered from 0 to n – 1.

Multidimensional Arrays

You can use arrays with more than one dimension in the C programming language. Take note that every dimension is represented as an array subscript. This means that a 2-dimensional array has two subscripts while a 3-dimensional array has three. An array can have any number of dimensions, depending on what is necessary. However, it is most likely that you will create an array with 1 or 2 dimensions.

For example, you declared a class called SQUARE. If you declare an array called Cardboard that represents it, you have to write:

SQUARE Cardboard [8] [8] ;

You can also represent this data using a 1-dimensional, 64-square array, such as in the following:

SQUARE Cardboard [64]

Multidimensional Array Initialization

You can initialize multidimensional arrays, as well as assign the list of values to the elements in the array in a certain order. You can do this as the last array subscript changes and all of the former stays in place. So if you write:

```
int theArray [ 5 ] [ 3 ]
```

You are commanding the first three elements to go to theArray [0] and the succeeding ones to go to theArray [1] and so on.

```
int theArray [ 5 ] [ 3 ] = { 1 , 2 , 3 , 4 , 5 , 6 , 7 , 8 , 9 , 10 , 11 , 12 , 13 , 14 , 15 }
```

To make everything much clearer, you can group your initializations using braces. Consider the following example:

```
int theArray [ 5 ] [ 3 ] = { { 1 , 2 , 3 } ,
{ 4 , 5 , 6 } ,
{ 7 , 8 , 9 } ,
{ 10 , 11 , 12 } ,
{ 13 , 14 , 15 } } ;
```

You have to take note that these inner braces are ignored by the compiler. It does not really matter if you use them or not, although they can help make your program appear more organized and clean.

So, if you want to make your program more effective, you should use braces instead. They represent the distribution of numbers. Do not forget to use a comma to separate the values, regardless of the presence of braces. Your entire initialization set has to be within the braces. Of course, your program has to end with a semicolon.

COMMENTS

Writing a program requires you to be careful and articulate. You need to make sure that your program is both executable and aesthetically pleasing. A messy program does not only cause errors, but it also results in confusion. For example, if you have been working on a particular program for so long, you may tend to forget some details. Thus, taking down notes is necessary.

The comments in programs seem to be nothing but unnecessary lines. However, they are actually necessary because they help bring clarity and organization to your program. Without them, your program may be unclear and confusing.

If a long time has passed since you last touched your program, you may forget some details. So, you need to include comments to help you stay on the right track and make your program presentable to other programmers or readers. The comments in C are merely texts that your system ignores. You can write anything in your comments sections.

Types of Comments

In general, the comments used in the C programming language are divided into two categories: double – slash (//) and slash – star (/*).

Double – slash comments, also known as C - style comments, tell your compiler to refrain from minding the things that follow them. Whatever you write after this comment, the compiler ignores. This process continues until it reaches the end of that particular line.

Slash – star comments, also known as C – style comments, tell your compiler to refrain from reading the things that follow them. The lines of text you write after the star – slash (*/) comment mark is not read by your computer. Always remember that each /* has to be paired with a closing */ .

In the C language, the C – style comment is also used. However, the C - style comment is not really a part of it. A lot of C programmers actually prefer to use the C - style comment in their work and only turn to the C – style comment to block out huge blocks in their program.

Using Comments

You can basically write comments all over your program. These comments can be anywhere. They are literally ignored by the compiler, so they will not do any harm to your program. Just make sure that you write your comments correctly. Do not be confused with the double – slash and the slash – star comments.

As a programmer, you are advised to put comments at the start of your programs so that you can clearly define what these programs do. The moment you read your program, you should immediately be able to tell what its purpose is. You should also be informed about its author, the date it was created, and even the time if that is included. You should also know about the functions used in the program.

Furthermore, statements in the program that are not that obvious must include comments so they can be noticed more easily. When you run your code, the process and the output stay the same. As you have learned, comments are pretty harmless.

Comments Seen at the Top of Every File

Ideally, you should include a comment block at the start of each file you make. Their style depends on your personal preference and/or requirements for the program. Nevertheless, you have to make sure that your headers include the necessary elements.

It has to include the name of your program or function as well as the name of the file. You also have to include the purpose of your program or function, plus a description or summary that explains how your program works.

In addition, you have to include your name but only if you are the author of the program. If there are any revisions made on the program, you have to include them as well. A history of these revisions, including the notes that you made on the changes, have to be included.

Furthermore, it has to include the liners, compilers, and other tools you used to create your program. If you have any other additional notes, you have to include them as well.

It is very important to keep descriptions and notes up to date. A lot of beginner programmers, and even advanced programmers, make the mistake of ignoring the comments section once they are done with their programs. They think that it is okay to leave the comments since the program is already working.

Once you complete your program, see to it that you still check their headers. Otherwise, your program can become misleading over time. Your readers can get confused because they are not aware that the headers are not up to date.

You have to keep in mind that comments can serve as invaluable guidelines to your overall program if only they are properly written and maintained. See to it that you check your program every now and then to update its header.

The // Comment versus the /* Style comment

When it comes to writing comments, you can choose between these two. The double – slash comment (//) expires by the end of the line while the slash – star (/*) comment stays in effect until the closing comment (*/) is reached. The slash – star comment cannot be terminated easily. Even when it reaches the end of the line, it may still continue until you place a closing comment mark. If you do not put this particular comment mark, you will encounter a compile – time error.

Bad Comments versus Good Comments

It should not really be difficult for you to tell apart bad comments from good comments. It is merely like telling a good fruit apart from a bad fruit.

A bad comment merely says the function of the code. It states what is already obvious. Even if you remove it, your program will still be the same. You can immediately tell if the comment is bad when you read the line of code and you already know what it is about. You may have understood what it is, what it does, and why it does it – yet it has a very minor effect on the program.

A good comment tells you why the code does whatever it does. It gives you a detailed explanation on why the program functions this way. It also explains what that particular code section is all about.

OTHER ELEMENTS

Statements

A program is basically a series of commands that are run according to a sequence. In the C programming language, the statements control the execution of the sequence. It also does the following: evaluate the expressions or even do nothing at all. The null statement is an example. All statements, including the null statement, have to end with a semicolon.

```
w = x + y;
```

In the example shown above, you can tell that *"the value of the sum of x and y is assigned to w."* Take note that this is not the same as in algebra wherein you read it as *w equals x + y.* In the C programming language, the assignment operators assign whatever elements are on the right with whatever elements are on the left.

Expressions

Expressions return values. They are also statements that you see in a program. You have to consider the following example:

```
PI                  // It is a float const that returns the
value 3.14
3.2                 // It returns the value 3.2
SecondsPerMinute    // It is an inst const that returns the
value 60
```

In the above given example, *PI* is a constant that is equivalent to *3.14* while *SecondsPerMinute* is another constant that is equivalent to *60.* These three statements are all expressions.

```
y = w + d ;
```

The above sample code is also an expression. It adds *w* and *d*, as well as allocates the resulting value to *y*. It also returns the value of the assignment.

```
w = d = x + y;
```

As you can see in the above given code, it is evaluated from *x* to *y*. The resulting value is then assigned to d, which in turn is assigned to w. If *w*, *d*, *x*, and *y* are integers, and *x* has a value of *3* while *y* has a value of 7, both *w* and *d* will be assigned with the value of *10*.

Keep in mind that your program has to store the data that it uses. Constants and variables have different ways of representing and manipulating data.

Defining Variables

The variable is the place where you put the information of your program. It is located in the memory of your computer. You can use it to store values that you can retrieve later on. This is great because you do not have to use a new variable every time.

The name of your variable is known as a label. For instance, you can use the variable name myVariableName. How many memory addresses there are depends on how big your variable name is.

Then, there is the RAM. It stands for random access memory. Every time you run a program, it gets loaded from disk to RAM. Every variable is also made in the RAM. In programming, the term *memory* is typically used to refer to the RAM of a computer.

Setting the Memory Aside

Before you start defining variables, you have to make sure that your compiler knows about this huge change. You have to inform it with regard to the type of variable used. You have to state if it is an integer or a character. Keep in mind that this information becomes the basis for determining how much room you have to reserve and what type of value you can use to store your variable in.

The type of variable that you use tells your compiler how much memory it has to reserve for such variable. Because the modern computers that people have today make use of bytes and bits when it comes to representing values, and since memory is usually measured in bytes, you have to take note of these concepts very carefully.

Integer Sizes

Every type of variable takes up a specific room amount. For example, an integer may be three bytes on a certain machine and three on another, but never changes when it is on either computer.

You can use the variable *char* to hold or store characters. Usually, it is a byte long while a short integer is a couple of bytes long. A *long* integer, on the other hand, tends to be four bytes while an integer that does not have the keywords *long* or *short* may be two or four bytes.

You should also learn about *character*, which takes up a byte of your computer's memory. It is usually a letter, symbol, or number.

Signed and Unsigned Integers

In nearly every program, you will see the word int. Integers are either signed or unsigned. You may need negative values at certain times, so you have to know what type of integer you need. Integers are generally assumed to be *signed*, unless they contain the word *unsigned*. This applies to both long and short integers.

Signed integers are either positive or negative. Unsigned integers, however, are always positive. Unsigned short integers can handle numbers between 0 and 65,535. Half of the numbers represented by signed short integers are negative. Signed short integers only have the capacity to represent numbers between -32,768 and 32,767.

Basic Variable Types

There are other variable types in the C programming language. These variable types may be divided conveniently into integer variables, character variables, and floating point variables. Floating point variables contain values that are allowed to be expressed as fractions. Then again, this is only possible if they are real numbers. Character variables can also contain a single byte. They are typically used for holding the two hundred and fifty-six symbols and characters of ASCII and its extended character sets.

The *ASCII character set* is a set of characters standardized to be used on computers. ASCII stands for American Standard Code for Information Interchange. Nearly every computer operating system in the world supports ASCII, and many of them support international character sets.

The variable types typically used in programs are written as follows. You will see the variable type and how much memory it takes up. You will also learn about the types of values that these variables can store. These values can be stored and determined through the size of their variable types.

Type	Size	Values
unsigned short int	2 bytes	0 to 65,535
short int	2 bytes	-32,768 to 32,767
unsigned long int	4 bytes	0 to 4,294,967,295
long int	4 bytes	-2,147,483,648 to 2,147,483,647
int (16 bit)	2 bytes	-32,768 to 32,767
int (32 bit)	4 bytes	-2,147,483,648 to 2,147,483,647
unsigned int (16 bit)	2 bytes	0 to 65,535
unsigned int (32 bit)	2 bytes	0 to 4,294,967,295
char	1 byte	256 character values
float	4 bytes	1.2e-38 to 3.4e38
double	8 bytes	2.2e-308 to 1.8e308

The sizes of your variables may not be exactly the same as the ones shown in the sample table above. Again, this can be a case-to-case basis. It depends on the computer and compiler that you have. If you get the same results, then the table applies to the compiler that you use. Otherwise, you should check out the manual of your compiler to see which values are held by your variable types.

Defining Variables

You define or create variables by stating the type, leaving at least one space, including its variable name, and closing it with a semicolon. For your variable name, you can use any letters. You can combine uppercase with lowercase letters. You can use numbers and then combine them with letters for your variable name. However, you should never include a space in your variables.

For example, *w*, *Wilson*, *W1lsoN*, and *wilsonn* are all legitimate variable names. Even if they have the same letters and number of characters, they are still considered to be different from one another. Also, even if you can use any variable name you want, make sure that you choose something that is beneficial to your program. You can choose a variable name that tells you and your readers what the program is about. For instance, if you are using an integer variable named *myAge :* , you can write it this way:

```
int myAge ;
```

A rule of thumb is to avoid using nonsense names such as *haFihDR93*. You cannot make any sense of it. It is just composed of random letters and numbers. It is hard to read and remember. In addition, you should avoid restricting your variable names to single letters only because they tend to cause confusion even if they are legitimate.

As much as possible, you should use variable names that already give a clue as to what the program is about. People should know what the program does even before they read the entire code or run the program. Expressive names like *myAge*, *SpeedLimit*, and *howMany* are all easy to understand and direct to the point. When you see these variable names, the first thing that comes to your mind may be to find out the age, speed limit, or number of a particular object in the program.

To help you understand this concept further, here's an example:

```
main ()
{
unsigned short a ;
unsigned short b ;
ULONG c ;
c = a * b ;
}
```

As you can see in the output shown above, the program performs the mathematical operation *multiplication*. You can see that the variable *c* is where the variable *a* is multiplied to the variable *b*. However, it is still unclear what these variables stand for. What exactly do *a*, *b*, and *c* represent? Are they units of measurement? Are they specific values? The lines of code do not make it clear what these variables are about. Therefore, these variable names are not ideal to be used in a program. Seeing this one for the first time may confuse you, especially if you do not have any previous experience with programming.

You have to take a look at another example:

```
main ()
{
unsigned short Area ;
unsigned short Length ;
unsigned short Width ;
Area = Length * Width ;
}
```

As you can see in the example shown above, it is clear that the variables represent the area, length, and width of a particular object. This program is much easier to read and understand than the previous one. The objective of the program is to find the area of a particular object by multiplying the length and width. It is straightforward, brief, and clear.

CHAPTER 5: POINTERS

C POINTERS

Pointers are amazing features of the C language. These features are what set this programming language apart from the others, including Python and Java. Pointers are used to manipulate addresses and access memory.

Address in the C Language

As a programmer, you have to familiarize yourself with the address used in the C language. You can use var, which is a variable in the program. You can also use &var, which gives you the address in your memory. Here, the notation & is referred to as the reference operator. You also need it if you have to use the function scanf ( ). It is necessary for the purpose of storing inputted values in the var address.

Take a look at the following code:

```
scanf ( "%d", &var ) ;
```

To help you understand this concept further, you should take a look at the following sample program:

```
/* This sample program demonstrates the usage of the reference operator in the C language. */
```

```c
#include < stdio.h >
int main ()
{
        int var = 5 ;
        printf ( "The value is %d \n " , var ) ;
        printf ( "The address is %u" , &var ) ;
// Check out the presence of the ampersand ( & ) character before
the var.
return 0 ;
}
```

When you run the above given sample program, you would get the following output:

The value is 5

The address is 2686778

You have to take note that you may get a different value for your address, depending on your computer. In the example shown above, a value of 5 gets stored in the 2686778 memory location. Var is used simply to provide a name to the location in the program.

Pointer Variables

In the C language, a special variable is used to store the address of another variable. This special variable is referred to as the pointer or the pointer variable.

Pointer Declaration

When you declare a pointer in your program, you can write the following codes:

```
data_type *  name_of_pointer_variable ;
int * p ;
```

As you can see in the sample statement shown above, p was defined as the pointer variable of the type int.

Reference and Deference Operators (& and *)

You can use two types of operators in your C programs: the reference operator & and the deference operator *. The previous operator provides you with the address of the variable, while the latter provides you with the value of this address.

To help you know more about pointers as well as deference operators and reference operators, you have to check out the following sample program. In this example, you will see how pointers work.

/* This is a source code that shows you how pointers are used in the C language */

```
#include < stdio.h >
int main ()
{
        int * pc ;
```

```
    int c ;
    c = 22 ;
    printf ( "The address of c is : %u \n " , &c ) ;
    printf ( "The value of c is : %d \n \n " , c ) ;
    pc = &c ;
    printf ("The address of the pointer is : %u \n " , pc ) ;
    printf ( "The content of the pointer pc is : %d \n \n " , *pc
) ;

    c = 11 ;
    printf ( "The address of the pointer pc is : %u \n ", pc ) ;
    printf ( "The content of the pointer pc : %d \n \n", *pc ) ;
    *pc = 2 ;
    printf ( "The address of c is : %u \n " , &c ) ;
    printf ( "The value of c is : %d \n \n " , c ) ;
    return 0;
}
```

When you run the above given example, you will get the following output:

```
The address of c is : 2686784
The value of c is : 22
The address of the pointer pc is : 2686784
The content of the pointer pc is : 22
The address of the pointer pc is : 2686784
The content of the pointer pc is : 11
The address of c is  2686784
The value of c is : 2
```

The above given sample program resulted in this output because of the following:

The command int * pc ; makes the pointer pc while the command int c ; makes the normal variable c. Because both c and pc are not initialized, the pointer pc can point to any random address or to no address at all.

Similarly, the variable c gets assigned a specific address even though it has a garbage value or random value.

A value of 22 gets assigned to the variable c because that is what you declared in the program when you wrote c = 22 ; . This stores the value 22 within the memory location of the variable c. You have to keep in mind that when you print &c, which refers to the address of c, you have to use %u instead of %d because the address is generally regarded as an unsigned integer. This makes it positive at all times.

The address of the variable c gets assigned to the pointer pc because you wrote pc = &c ; . When it comes to printing, the value of the pointer is the same as the address of the variable. In this case, the value of pc is similar to that of the address of c. In addition, the content of the pointer pc is also the value 22.

Then, the value 11 gets assigned to the variable c because you wrote c = 11 ; . You have to allocate a new value to the variable c in order for you to see how it affects the pointer pc.

Due to the fact that the pointer pc also points to the address of the variable c, the value that the pointer pc uses is also 11. When you print the content and the address of pc, you display the updated content.

Everything that the memory location contains is changed when you use *pc = 2 ; . The pointer pc points towards the value 2. Because the address of the pointer is similar to that of the variable c, the value of c changes to 2 as well.

Frequently Asked Questions (FAQ)

What are the common mistakes that programmers make when they work with pointers?

A lot of programmers make a mistake when they use pointers to point to the addresses of variables.

For instance, they make a mistake when declaring the pointer and the address, such as in the following sample code:

```
int c , *pc ;
pc = c ;
```

In the above given example, pc is used as an address. However, the same cannot be said of c because it is not an address.

Here is another example:

```
int c , *pc ;
*pc = &c ;
```

In the above given example, the address points to the value *pc while &c ; is the address.

So, what are the correct codes to be used then?

Take a look at the following example:

```
int c , * pc ;
pc = &c ;
```

In the above given example, both &pc and pc are addresses.

```
int c , *pc ;
*pc = c ;
```

Lastly, the above given example shows that the address points to *pc, with c also being a value.

In both of these cases, the pointer pc does not point to the address of the variable c.

Arrays and Pointers

Arrays are in close relation with the pointers in the C language. However, even though they are related, they are still different from each other. For instance, the pointer variable has a different address for every value while the array only has a fixed one.

To understand this concept further, you have to take a look at the following sample program:

```
#include < stdio.h >
int main ()
{
        char charArray [ 4 ] ;
        int i ;

for ( i = 0 ; i < 4 ; ++ i )
{
        printf ( " The address of the charArray [ %d ] is %u \n " , i
, &charArray [ i ] ;
}

return 0 ;
}
```

When you run the above given sample program, you will see the following output:

```
The address of the charArray [ 0 ] is 28ff44

The address of the charArray [ 1 ] is 28ff45

The address of the charArray [ 2 ] is 28ff46

The address of the charArray [ 3 ] is 28ff47
```

You have to take note that there is a possibility for you to get a different address for the array that you used in your program.

Also, you have to be observant with regard to the differences of bytes between the consecutive elements of the arrays. In the above given example, there is an obvious difference of one byte between the two elements that are consecutive in the array charArray.

However, because the pointers simply point towards the location of a new variable, it has the capability to store whatever address there is.

The Relationship of Pointers and Arrays

You have to remember that in the C language, the name of an array points to the address of the array's first element at all times. Take a look at the following example:

```
int arr [ 4 ] ;
```

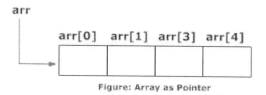

Figure: Array as Pointer

As you can see in the above given example, the arrays arr [0] and arr both point to the address of the declared first element. In this example, arr is equivalent to &arr [0].

Because their addresses are similar, their values are similar as well. If you will study both &arr [0] and arr, you will see that they have the same values.

*arr is equivalent to arr [0] in terms of the value of the addresses of their pointers.

Likewise, you can say that &arr [1] has the same equivalence as (arr + 1). At the same time arr [1] and *(arr + 1) have the same equivalence. Then, &arr [2] has the same equivalence as (arr + 2) while at the same time, arr [2] has the same equivalence as *(arr + 2). Also, &arr [3] has the same equivalence as (arr + 3) while at the same time, arr [3] has the same equivalence as *(arr + 3). This pattern goes on and on until you reach &arr [i], which has the same equivalence as (arr + i). At the same time, arr [i] has the same equivalence as *(arr + i).

Keep in mind that in the C language, you are free to declare arrays and use pointers to change the data of your arrays.

To better understand this concept, you have to take a look at the following sample program. In this program, you will see how you can get the sum of six numbers with pointers and arrays.

```c
#include < stdio.h >
int main ()
{
        int i , classes [ 6 ] , sum = 0 ;
        printf ( " You have to enter six numbers :  \n " ) ;
        for ( i = 0 ; i < 6 ; ++i )
{

        // In this sample program, you have to take note that (
classes + i ) has the same equivalence as &classes [ i ]

        scanf ( " %d " , ( classes + i ) ) ;

        // In this sample program, you have to take note that *(
classes + i ) has the same equivalence as classes [ i ]

        sum += *( classes + i ) ;
}
printf ( " The sum of the numbers is equal to :  %d " , sum ) ;
return 0 ;
}
```

When you run the above given sample program, you will get the following output:

You have to enter six numbers :

3

2

1

7

3

5

The sum of the numbers is equal to : 21

In the above given sample program, you are asked to enter six numbers because that is what has been declared. You are free to input any number you want. They do not have to be in a certain order or follow a specific sequence. You just have to enter six numbers. Once you are done entering the six numbers, the program will compute their sum because that is what was declared. Whatever value was computed will be displayed in the output.

If you are still having a bit of a hard time understanding this concept, you have to take a look at the following sample program. In this other example, you will learn how you can access the elements of an array with the use of pointers.

```
#include < stdio.h >
int main ()
{
        int data [ 5 ] , i ;
        printf ( " You have to input elements here : " ) ;
        for ( i = 0 ; i < 5 ; ++i )
        scanf ( " %d " , data + i ) ;
        printf ( " You have entered the elements : \n " ) ;
        for ( i = 0 ; i < 5 ; ++i )
        printf ( " %d \n " , *( data + i ) ) ;
return 0 ;
}
```

When you run the above given sample program, you will get the following output:

You have to input elements here : 5

6

7

9

8

You have entered the elements :

5

6

7

9

8

As you can see in the above given example, the elements used are kept in an integer array data. With the use of a for loop, every one of the elements in the data is passed through and printed with the use of a pointer technique.

Functions and Pointers

The moment the pointer gets passed to the function as an argument, the address of its memory location gets passed rather than its value.

To help you understand the concept of functions and pointers better, here's another sample program. In this example, you will see how two numbers are swapped with the use of a call by reference.

```c
/* This is an example of a program in the C language that swaps
two numbers with the use of functions and pointers. */

#include < stdio.h >
void swap ( int *n1 , int *n2 ) ;

int main ()
{
        int num1 = 5 , num2 = 10 ;

// The addresses of num1 and num2, respectively, are passed on to
the function swap

        swap ( &num1, &num2 ) ;
        printf ( " The value of num1 is : %d \n " , num1 ) ;
        printf ( " The value of num2 is : %d " , num2 ) ;
        return 0 ;
}

void swap ( int * n1 , int * n2 )
{

// The pointers n1 and n2, respectively, points towards the
addresses of num1 and num2

        int temp ;
        temp = *n1 ;
        *n1 = *n2 ;
        *n2 = temp ;
}
```

If you run the above given sample program, you will obtain the following output:

The value of num1 is 10

The value of num2 is 5

As you can see in the output, the addresses of the memory locations num1 and num2, respectively, are passed on towards the function swap as well as the pointers *n1 and *n2, respectively. The values are accepted. Thus, the pointers n1 and n2 now point to the addresses of num1 and num2.

In case the values of the pointers are switched, the value indicated within the specific memory location changes as well. Therefore, whatever changes are made to both *n1 and *n2 are shown in both num1 and num2 at the function main. In the C language, such technique is referred to as call by reference.

To help you understand this concept further, you have to consider the following examples.

Use Call By Reference to Swap Numbers In a Cyclic Order

This sample program shows you how pointers are used to collect integers and swap them in a cyclic order.

As the user, you have to input three variables. The values that you entered will be stored in their respective locations, which in this case, are variables a, b, and c.

The variables will be passed on towards the function cyclicSwap ( ). Rather than pass the actual variables, the addresses of the variables are the ones that are passed. Once these variables get swapped in a cyclic order in the function cyclicSwap ( ), the variables a, b, and c within the function main also gets swapped automatically.

In order for you to understand this concept further, you have to take a look at the following example. In this sample program, you will see how elements are swapped with the use of the call by reference.

```c
#include < stdio.h >
void cyclicSwap ( int *a , int * b , int * c ) ;

int main ()
{
        int a , b , c ;
printf ( " You have to enter a value for a, b, and c : " ) ;
scanf ( " %d %d %d " , &a , &b, &c ) ;

printf ( " You have to enter a value before you swap \n " ) ;
printf ( " a = %d \n b = %d \n c = %d \n " , a, b, c ) ;
cyclicSwap ( &a , &b, &c ) ;
printf ( " The value after swapping is \n " ) ;
printf ( " a = %d \n b = %d \n c = %d " , a , b , c ) ;
return 0 ;
}

void cyclicSwap ( int * a , int * b , int * c )
{
int temp ;

// This sample shows how swapping is done in a cyclic order

temp = *b ;
*b = *a ;
*a = *c ;
*c = temp ;

}
```

When you run the above given sample program, you will get the following output:

You have to enter the value for a, b, and c : 1

2

3

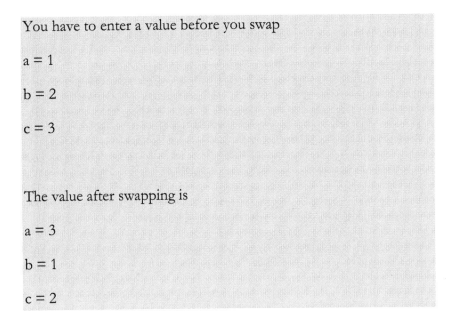

You have to enter a value before you swap

a = 1

b = 2

c = 3

The value after swapping is

a = 3

b = 1

c = 2

As you can see, there were no values that have been returned from the function cyclicSwap ( ).

MEMORY MANAGEMENT

In the C programming language, you can dynamically allocate the memory with the use of standard library functions. These include malloc ( ) , free ( ) , realloc ( ) , and calloc ( ).

Also, in the C programming language, the exact array size remains unknown until the compile time occurs. This compile time is about the compiler compiling the code into a language that is easy to understand.

Through dynamic memory allocation, your program can acquire a bigger memory space as it runs. Conversely, it allows it to have more memory to release if it does not need it. Simply put, dynamic memory allocation lets you manually deal with the memory space in the program.

Even though this programming language does not have an inherent technique for allocating memory dynamically, you can use library functions.

Function	Usage
malloc ( )	It allocates the requested size of the bytes and then returns the pointer first byte of the allocated space
calloc ( )	It allocates the space for the elements of an array. It also initializes to zero and returns the pointer to memory
realloc ( )	It changes the size of the previously allocated space
free ( )	It deallocates the previously allocated space

Malloc ( )

It stands for memory allocation. This function reserves memory and returns the pointer type of void. Its syntax is as follows:

ptr = (cast – type *) malloc (byte – size)

ptr is the cast-type pointer. The pointer is returned by the malloc ( ) function to an area of the memory. If there is not enough space, the allocation does not occur and the NULL pointer is returned. Consider the following example:

ptr = (int *) malloc (100 * sizeof (int)) ;

Calloc ( )

It stands for contiguous allocation. It is different from malloc ( ) in the way that it allocates multiple memory blocks that have the same size whereas malloc ( ) allocates single memory blocks. This function also sets the bytes to zero. Its syntax is as follows:

ptr = (cast – type *) calloc (n , element – size) ;

The statement allocates a contiguous space in the memory for the array of n elements. Consider the following example:

ptr = (float *) calloc (25 , sizeof (float)) ;

Realloc ( )

It can be used to change the previously allocated size of the memory in case there is too little or too much of it. Its syntax is as follows:

```
ptr = realloc ( ptr , newsize ) ;
```

ptr gets reallocated with the size of newsize.

Free ( )

It is used to release the space or free a dynamically-allocated memory that was created using malloc ( ) or calloc ( ). Its syntax is as follows:

```
free ( ptr ) ;
```

It frees the space that was allocated in the memory that ptr pointed to.

CONCLUSION:

I hope this book was able to help you learn about the C programming language. All that's left for you to do is apply everything you have learned.

While successfully creating your own "Hello World!" application might not seem like a great feat, everything needs to start somewhere. Maximize your learning experience and try every example provided in this book. Also, don't hesitate to write your own programs and experiment with the different functions.

Getting creative with the programming language is among the best ways to familiarize yourself with the many possibilities that it offers. Even if you're not planning to become an expert in C, your time and effort studying it won't be wasted – after all, the more you learn about it, the more capable you become in handling other languages.

So, what are you waiting for? Further expand your knowledge of the programming language through regular practice and by giving in to your curiosity.

Thank you so much for taking the time to read this book. Good luck and may you succeed in your programming pursuits!

OTHER BOOKS BY AUTHOR NAME

Book 1 Description here.

Book 1 Link

Book 2 Description here.

Book 2 Link

Book 3 Description here.

Book 3 Link

DID YOU ENJOY THIS BOOK?

I want to thank you for purchasing and reading this book. I really hope you got a lot out of it.

Can I ask a quick favor though?

If you enjoyed this book I would really appreciate it if you could leave me a positive review on Amazon.

I love getting feedback from my customers and reviews on Amazon really do make a difference. I read all my reviews and would really appreciate your thoughts.

Thanks so much.

AUTHOR NAME

p.s. You can click here to go directly to the book on Amazon and leave your review.

Other Books From This Author

1) *Python Programming: Your Guide To Easily Learn Python Programming in 7 Days*

2) *Java Programming: Your Guide To Easily Learn Java Programming in 7 Days*

3) *Html and Css For Beginners: Your Guide To Easily Learn Html and Css Programming in 7 Days*

4) *Programming For Beginners: 3 Manuscripts in 1 Bundle - Python For Beginners, Java Programming and Html & CSS For Beginners*

5) *Html5 and Css3 For Beginners: Your Guide To Easily Learn Html5 and Css3 Programming in 7 Days*

6) *C Programming: Your Guide To Easily Learn C Programming in 7 Days*

7) *SQL For Beginners: Your Guide To Easily Learn SQL Programming in 7 Days*

Made in the USA
Middletown, DE
02 March 2018